Common Edible and Poisonous Mushrooms of New York

Alan E. Bessette

&

Arleen R. Bessette

Syracuse University Press

Copyright © 2006 by Syracuse University Press
Syracuse, New York, 13244–5160

All Rights Reserved

First Edition 2006
06 07 08 09 10 11   6 5 4 3 2 1

Publication of this book is made possible by a grant from Furthermore:
a program of the J. M. Kaplan Fund.

It is also supported in part with a grant from The Greenwald
Haupt Vision Fund, Harry R. Greenwald, director.

Unless otherwise stated, all photographs courtesy of the authors.

The paper used in this publication meets the minimum
requirements of American National Standard for Information
Sciences—Permanence of Paper for Printed Library Materials,
ANSI Z39.48–1984.∞™

Library of Congress Cataloging-in-Publication Data
Bessette, Alan.
Common edible and poisonous mushrooms of New York / Alan E. Bessette and
Arleen R. Bessette.— 1st ed.
p. cm.
Includes bibliographical references (p.) and index.
ISBN 0–8156–0848–9 (pbk. : alk. paper)
1. Mushrooms—New York (State)—Identification. 2. Mushrooms, Poisonous—New
York (State)—Identification. I. Bessette, Arleen Rainis, 1951– II. Title.
QK605.5.N7B47 2006
579.6'163209747—dc22   2006005293

Manufactured in Canada

This book has been written to eliminate or minimize the possibility of experiencing adverse reactions when consuming wild mushrooms. However, no amount of knowledge or experience can make the consumption of wild mushrooms totally risk-free. Misidentification, individual sensitivities or allergies, and contamination are beyond our control. When properly used, this book will minimize the danger of accidental poisoning; however, neither the authors nor the publisher can accept any responsibility for adverse reactions that may result from eating wild mushrooms.

Contents

Preface   ix

Acknowledgments   x

Introduction   1
- Mushroom Basics   1
- Collecting Mushrooms for the Table   2
- How to Make a Spore Print   3
- How to Use This Guide   4
- Mushroom Identification Procedure   4

Color Key to the Major Groups of Mushrooms   7

Descriptions and Illustrations of Edible Species   17
- Boletes   17
- Chanterelles and Allies   20
- Coral Fungi   24
- Gilled Mushrooms   26
- Giant Puffballs   44
- *Hypomyces*   46
- Morels   48
- Polypores   50
- Tooth Fungi   54

Descriptions and Illustrations of Inedible and Poisonous Species   59
- Boletes   59
- False Morels   64
- Gilled Mushrooms   66

The Culinary Mushroom 81

    Guidelines for Eating Wild Mushrooms 81

    Preparing and Preserving Wild Mushrooms 82

    Cooking Wild Mushrooms 83

    Wild Mushroom Recipes 84

Glossary 99

Recommended Reading 103

Index to Common Names 105

Index to Scientific Names 107

Preface

Gathering wild mushrooms for the table is often viewed in North America as a dangerous hobby that should be avoided. A common perception exists that most mushrooms are poisonous and very difficult to identify. It is true that there are several poisonous species and that some mushrooms are difficult to identify. However, many mushrooms are excellent edibles and are easy to identify. This book focuses on some of the easy-to-identify edible species found in New York State. We have taken great care to provide the reader with key identifying features and color illustrations to identify each edible species positively. In addition, we have provided descriptions and illustrations of any poisonous or inedible species with which the edible mushrooms may be confused because they are similar.

This book is not a field guide that attempts to identify most of the mushrooms you may encounter. Unlike most popular mushroom field guides, it does emphasize the identification of edible wild mushrooms. Although it contains seven recipes, it is not intended to be a mushroom cookbook. A list of recommended field guides and mushroom cookbooks is provided in the section titled "Recommended Reading."

The purpose of this book is to introduce you to the fascinating and enjoyable pastime of gathering and eating wild mushrooms. It has been designed and written to make mushroom gathering and eating a safe and rewarding experience. We hope that it will bring countless hours of enjoyment to those who use it.

Acknowledgments

We thank Dail Dunaway for allowing us to include his photograph of *Hericium erinaceus* and Sam Norris for the use of his mushroom illustration in the introduction. Our appreciation also goes to Annie Barva, who painstakingly copyedited the manuscript. Special thanks to Peter Webber and his staff at Syracuse University Press for making this book possible.

Common Edible and Poisonous Mushrooms of New York

Introduction

Mushroom Basics

Mushrooms are classified in the kingdom Fungi. They lack chlorophyll and cannot manufacture food for themselves. Mushrooms obtain nourishment by secreting enzymes externally on a *substrate,* a food source, and absorbing the digested nutrients. Some mushrooms called *saprobes* extract nutrients from dead and decaying matter. Others, called *parasites,* attack living plants, animals, or other fungi. A third group participate in a mutually beneficial relationship with living trees or other plants, called a *mycorrhizal relationship* or *mycorrhiza.* Each partner that participates in a mycorrhizal relationship benefits and obtains what it needs, in part, from the other.

Mushrooms consist of a *mycelium:* a vast network of microscopic threadlike filaments. The mycelium develops in soil, decaying wood, leaf litter, dung, or a variety of other substrates. When conditions such as temperature, moisture, and daylight length are favorable, the mycelium produces a *fruit body,* a visible mushroom. The fruit body produces microscopic reproductive structures called *spores.*

An immature mushroom is called a *button.* The button of some mushroom species may be completely surrounded by a membranous structure called the *universal veil.* When the mushroom expands, it stretches and tears the universal veil, often leaving remnants on the cap. These remnants are referred to as *patches* or *warts.* Sometimes a *volva,* a cuplike remnant of the universal veil, surrounds the base of the mushroom stalk. Most mushrooms lack a universal veil and therefore also lack cap remnants and a volva.

A typical mature mushroom has a *cap* and *stalk.* The stalk may be attached to the center of the cap or at the side of the cap. The underside of the cap may have *gills,* knifebladelike structures on which spores are formed. Instead of gills, the underside of some mushrooms have *teeth/spines* or vertically arranged, closely packed *tubes.* If tubes are present, the open end of each tube is called a *pore,* and the collective pores are called the *pore surface.* Both teeth/spines and

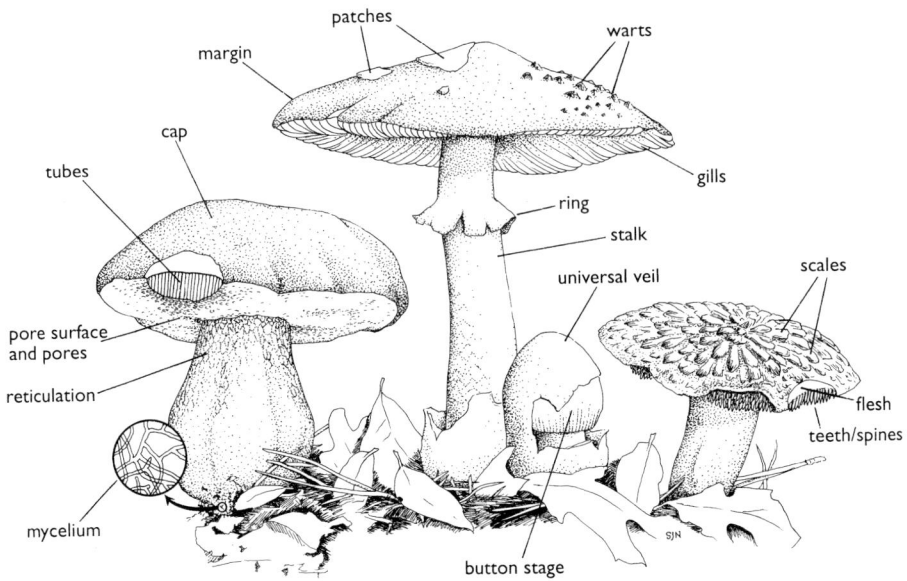

Parts of a Mushroom. Drawing by Sam Norris.

tubes serve the same basic reproductive function as gills. In some species, the underside of the immature cap is covered by a piece of tissue stretching from the cap's edge, or *margin,* to the stalk. This tissue, the *partial veil* (not shown), covers and protects the developing gills or tubes. As the mushroom cap expands, the partial veil tears, often leaving remnants on the cap margin or adhering to the stalk, where it forms a *ring.*

Collecting Mushrooms for the Table

Unlike hobbies or pastimes that require expensive equipment, collecting mushrooms for the table requires only a few simple, inexpensive items: a basket or other sturdy container in which to place your collections; a sturdy, sharp knife; waxed paper or paper bags; and comfortable clothing appropriate to weather and terrain. Other useful items include insect repellant, a compass, a walking stick, a notepad, a pen, and food and beverage.

There are two recommended methods for collecting wild mushrooms for the table. If you are certain of the identification, gather the mushrooms by cutting the stalks above the substrate and placing them in a container. This type of gathering minimizes the amount of debris that will need to be removed at a later time. If you are uncertain about the identification of a species and choose to gather it for identification, be sure to collect all parts of the fruit body. Whenever possible, gather mushrooms in all stages of development and add a note to the collection that describes the substrate and habitat where the species was collected. It is important to keep each species collection separate to avoid confusion and possible misidentification. Carefully wrap each collection in waxed paper or paper bags. If the collection is large and more than one sheet of waxed paper or one bag is required, include a note identifying each collection. Do not use plastic bags or plastic wrap because they trap moisture, which hastens spoilage.

The type of mushroom you wish to gather often determines where you are likely to collect it. Knowing whether a mushroom is mycorrhizal with a specific tree species or the type of substrate it requires for growth can be very important in determining where to look for a particular species. The Fruiting section of each description provides information about the habitat where each mushroom is likely to occur.

It is impossible to predict exactly when mushrooms will fruit because several factors affect this process, including precipitation, humidity, temperature, and daylight length. Some mushrooms fruit only once a season, whereas others have split or multiple fruiting periods. The best time to collect is usually three to five days after a significant rainfall or sooner if rains have been falling at frequent intervals. Information describing the period when a mushroom is likely to fruit is given in the Fruiting section of each description.

How to Make a Spore Print

Obtaining a spore print is an important step in the mushroom identification process. The color of the spore print is often a key identification feature, so it is important to know how to make a print.

Although it is often not necessary to make a spore print when identifying an unknown mushroom, a print can prevent misidentification of species. Some species similar to edible species may be poisonous. For example, determining the white spore print of the edible Honey Mushroom will prevent confusion with the Deadly Galerina, which has a brown spore print.

To make a spore print, cut the stalk squarely off close to the cap leaving about a $1/2$" stub to serve as a pedestal. Place the cap with the gills, teeth/spines, or pores down on a piece of white paper and cover it with an inverted cup or bowl or similar container to restrict air currents. Allow several hours or overnight if necessary for the spores to fall on the paper. Remove the cover and then the mushroom cap and observe the color of the spore print in natural light.

How to Use This Guide

The mushroom species illustrated in this book are arranged alphabetically within major groups based on similarities in their appearance. Representatives of each of the ten major groups are illustrated in the Color Key to the Major Groups of Mushrooms. The color key and accompanying brief descriptions constitute the foundation upon which this guide is based.

If you know the identification of a species and wish to read about it, consult the index. If, however, you wish to identify an unknown mushroom, follow the mushroom identification procedure presented in the book. Before attempting the identification procedure, however, be sure that you have collected as many different stages of the mushroom as possible in as *fresh* condition as possible, made notes about the habitat and substrate, and obtained a spore print if one is obtainable. Identifying mushrooms can sometimes be a difficult task, and every bit of information is useful.

Mushroom Identification Procedure

1. Always start at the beginning of the color key and determine which major group best describes the mushroom you are attempting to identify.
2. Turn to the page indicated for the major group and read the introductory information presented.
3. Examine the color illustrations provided for the major group and compare them with your unknown. Then read the specific descriptions of species within that group to find any that appear

to match your unknown. Be sure to read the Comments section for additional information.
4. When determining the identification of an unknown species, *make sure that every key identification feature listed in the description is consistent with your unknown mushroom!*
5. If you are unable to identify the mushroom positively, or if any of the key identifying features is not in agreement with your mushroom, or if you have any doubt about your identification, *do not eat the mushroom!*

Color Key to the Major Groups of Mushrooms

Boletes (see pp. 17, 59)

Fleshy fruit body with cap and typically central stalk; cap undersurface with a spongelike layer of vertically arranged tubes, each terminating in a pore; the spongelike layer usually separates easily from the cap tissue; growing on the ground or sometimes on wood.

Boletus edulis, see p. 18

Tylopilus felleus, see p. 62

Chanterelles and Allies (see p. 20)

Fleshy fruit body with cap and stalk, or funnel-like shape; undersurfaces with blunt, gill- to veinlike ridges that are often forked and crossveined, or nearly smooth; usually growing on the ground.

Cantharellus lateritius, see p. 21

Cantharellus cinnabarinus, see p. 21

Coral Fungi (see p. 24)

Fruit body erect, coral-like, with repeatedly branched appendages; growing on the ground or on wood.

Clavicorona pyxidata, see p. 24

Ramaria concolor, see p. 25

False Morels (see p. 64)

Cap brainlike, saddle shaped, or irregularly lobed; stalk typically multichambered; growing on the ground or on decaying wood.

Gyromitra esculenta, see p. 64

Gyromitra infula, see p. 49

Gilled Mushrooms (see pp. 26, 66)

Undersurfaces with knifebladelike gills radiating from a stalk, or on stalkless species from point of attachment to the substrate; growing on a variety of substrates.

Agaricus arvensis, see p. 27

Lactarius corrugis, see p. 37

Giant Puffballs (see p. 44)

Large rounded fruit body that measures 4–24" in diameter; outer covering white to pale brown, with a texture that feels like deerskin; growing on the ground in woodlands or in grassy habitats.

Langermania gigantea, see p. 44

Calvatia cyathiformis, see p. 45

Hypomyces (see p. 46)

Parasitic fungi that attack and usually disfigure gilled mushrooms, boletes, polypores, and other fungi; each has a roughened, sandpaperlike, moldy, feathery, or powdery appearance and texture.

Hypomyces lactifluorum, see p. 46

Hypomyces luteovirens, see p. 47

Morels (see p. 48)

Fruit body with conic to bell-shaped cap that has pits and ridges; stalks typically hollow and not multichambered; growing on the ground.

Morchella esculenta, see p. 48

Morchella semilibera, see p. 49

Polypores (see p. 50)

Woody conks and fleshy to leathery mushrooms with pores on their undersurfaces (the pores are sometimes minute; use a hand lens); the pore layer typically does not separate easily from the cap tissue; shape varies from including cap and stalk to being stalkless and shelflike, or rather complex; growing on wood or sometimes on the ground arising from buried wood.

Laetiporus sulphureus, see p. 52

Meripilus sumstinei, see p. 51

Tooth Fungi (see p. 54)

Fleshy, corky, or leathery mushrooms with downward-oriented spines or teeth; shape varies from including cap and stalk to being branched and iciclelike, fan shaped, or shelflike; growing on the ground, on wood, or on fallen pine cones.

Hydnum umbilicatum, see p. 57

Hericium americanum, see p. 55

Descriptions and Illustrations of Edible Species

Boletes

Boletes, also known as *fleshy pored fungi,* are among the most fascinating and highly prized mushrooms. Their beautiful colors, distinctive features, excellent flavor and texture, and common occurrence make them one of the most popular groups collected. Boletes are a safe group to collect for the table and are immensely popular among mycophiles and mycophagists. Most boletes grow on the ground and are soft and fleshy. They have a cap, a stalk, and a spongelike layer of tubes on the undersurface of the cap. They also have vertically arranged tubes, each of which terminates in a pore. The tube layer is easily detached and typically separates cleanly from the cap flesh.

Boletes can safely be collected for consumption provided three important rules are followed. First, *do not* eat boletes whose pore surfaces are orange to red. Second, avoid boletes that stain blue to grayish blue, greenish blue, or blackish when cut or bruised. Third, avoid boletes that have bitter-tasting flesh.

A similar group called *polypores* also have tubes, but can easily be differentiated from boletes because most of the former grow on wood. Although some polypores are edible, the fruit bodies of most are typically tough and leathery to woody, and their tube layers usually do not separate cleanly from the cap flesh.

Boletus edulis

Scientific name: *Boletus edulis*

Common name: King Bolete, Cep, Porcini

Key identifying features

1. Cap some shade of brown to rusty red or yellowish tan.
2. Pore surface white to yellow; not pink, orange, or red.
3. All parts of the mushroom not blueing when cut or bruised.
4. Cap flesh white, mild tasting.
5. Stalk white to pale brownish, with a whitish netlike pattern over the upper portion or nearly overall.

Cap: $1^{3}/_{4}$–10" wide, convex to nearly flat; surface smooth to slightly wrinkled, dry, sticky when wet; brown to reddish brown, pale cinnamon-brown, rusty red, or yellowish tan; flesh white, not blueing when bruised; odor and taste not distinctive.

Pore surface: white when young, becoming yellow to olive-yellow then brownish yellow to brown in age, staining yellowish olive to dull orange-cinnamon or pale yellowish brown when bruised.

Stalk: 2–10" long, $3/4$–3" thick, enlarging downward or nearly equal; sometimes bulbous, white or pale brown, with a distinct whitish net on the upper one-third or more; solid; partial veil and ring absent.

Spore print: olive-brown.

Fruiting: solitary, scattered, or in groups on the ground in woods, especially under conifers; June-October; fairly common.

Edibility: edible and choice; one of the most highly prized edible mushrooms.

Comments: The Bitter Bolete, *Tylopilus felleus,* inedible, has a brown stalk with a coarse, dark brown net on its stalk and very bitter-tasting flesh (see p. 62). Several poisonous boletes, including the Red-mouth Bolete, *Boletus subvelutipes,* have a red to orange pore surface and yellow flesh that rapidly stains blue when cut or bruised (see p. 60).

Chanterelles and Allies

Members of this small group produce fruit bodies that are often funnel- to vase-shaped at maturity. Many resemble gilled mushrooms, but their spores are not produced on true gills. Their fertile surfaces are typically blunt, gill- to veinlike ridges that are often forked or joined together by crossveins, and a few have a nearly smooth fertile surface. Chanterelles usually grow on the ground. Many are popular edibles.

Cantharellus cibarius

Scientific name: *Cantharellus cibarius*

Common name: Golden Chanterelle

Key identifying features

1. Yellow to golden yellow or orange-yellow smooth cap.
2. Cap edge incurved to inrolled when young, often wavy in age.
3. Stalk pale yellow to orange-yellow, solid.

4. Undersurface of cap with forked, blunt, gill-like ridges, lacking true thin-edged gills.
5. Growing on the ground scattered or in groups or sometimes in small fused clusters.

Cap: $5/8$–$5 1/2$" wide, convex to nearly plane, sometimes with a depressed center; surface dry, nearly smooth, orange-yellow to yellow; margin thin, incurved to inrolled when young, often remaining so for a long time, becoming uplifted and wavy in age, sometimes crimped or lobed.

Flesh: thick, firm, white; odor fragrant like apricots or not distinctive; taste peppery or not distinctive.

Fertile surface: decurrent, with forked, blunt, gill-like ridges, with or without crossveins, pale yellow to yellow or pale orange.

Stalk: $5/8$–$2 3/4$" long, up to 1" thick, equal or enlarged at either end; smooth, pale yellow to orange-yellow.

Spore print: pinkish cream to pale buff.

Fruiting: solitary, scattered, in groups, or sometimes clustered on the ground in woods; July–September; fairly common.

Edibility: edible, choice.

Comments: The Smooth Chanterelle, *Cantharellus lateritius,* edible, is nearly identical except that the undersurface of the cap is nearly smooth (see p. 8). The Cinnabar-red Chanterelle, *Cantharellus cinnabarinus,* edible, is similar, but it has a smaller reddish orange cap and stalk, and pale reddish orange to orange-salmon gill-like ridges (see p. 8). Also compare with the Jack O'Lantern, *Omphalotus olearius,* poisonous, which has true gills with sharp edges and grows on wood or buried wood, typically in large overlapping clusters (see p. 78).

Craterellus fallax

Scientific name: *Craterellus fallax*

Common name: Black Trumpet

Key identifying features

1. Vase- or trumpet-shaped mushroom with thin, brittle flesh, often with a pleasant fruity or fragrant odor.
2. Fruit body 2–5" tall.
3. Stalk hollow, flaring open at the top.
4. Upper surface some shade of dark brown to blackish, usually with radiating fibers or tiny scales.
5. Fertile surface smooth or with veinlike ridges, grayish to brownish or blackish, often with ochraceous orange tints.
6. Growing on the ground in moist hardwoods or mixed woodlands.

Cap: $^3/_8$–$3^1/_8$" wide, funnel shaped, and deeply depressed; upper surface grayish brown to dark brown or blackish, with darker radiating fibers or tiny fibrous scales; margin inrolled at first, becoming arched, wavy, and irregular.

Flesh: thin, brittle to fibrous, colored like the surface; odor pleasant, often somewhat fruity or fragrant; taste not distinctive.

Fertile surface: decurrent, smooth or with shallow, blunt, veinlike ridges, gray to brown or blackish, often with ochraceous orange tints, bruising blackish.

Stalk: indistinct, a short extension below the fertile surface, often hollow, dark brown to blackish.

Spore print: ochraceous orange to ochraceous buff.

Fruiting: scattered or in groups or clusters on the ground in hardwoods or mixed woods; July–September; occasional to fairly common.

Edibility: edible and very popular.

Comments: This mushroom is an excellent choice for drying and grinding into powder; powdered mushroom adds a distinctive flavor to meats, fish, and vegetable dishes.

Coral Fungi

Coral fungi are species with erect, repeatedly branched, coral-like stalks that grow solitary or in groups. Most species have brittle flesh and are easily broken, but some are fibrous to tough and flexible. Most species grow on the ground, but some can be found on decaying wood or on the bark of standing trees. Several species are edible; some are poisonous; and the others are inedible or of unknown edibility. Similar species with downward-oriented spines are included in the tooth fungi.

Clavicorona pyxidata

Scientific name: *Clavicorona pyxidata*

Common name: Crown-tipped Coral

Key identifying features

1. Fruit body growing on decaying hardwood.
2. Fruit body erect and coral-like, with repeatedly forked branches.

3. Branch tips distinctly crownlike.
4. Fruit body white to pale creamy white when young, becoming ochre-yellow or tan in age.

Fruit body: up to $5^{1}/_{8}$" high, erect and coral-like, with numerous repeatedly forked branches arising from a short stalk; branch tips distinctly crownlike; surface smooth, white to pale creamy white when young, becoming ochre-yellow or tan in age; flesh tough to brittle, whitish; odor usually not distinctive; taste somewhat peppery.

Spore print: white.

Fruiting: solitary, scattered, or in groups on decaying hardwoods; June-September; fairly common.

Edibility: edible.

Comments: *Ramaria concolor,* inedible, is similar and also grows on decaying wood, but it has pointed branch tips that lack the distinctive crown, and it has a strongly aromatic odor (see p. 9). There are many other species of coral fungi. Most grow on the ground, and the remaining few species grow on wood. No other coral fungi that grow on wood have the distinctive crownlike branch tips found on the Crown-tipped Coral.

Gilled Mushrooms

Gilled mushrooms belong to a very large group of fungi that have caps with knifebladelike gills on the undersurface. Many have a central stalk, whereas others are eccentrically to laterally stalked or stalkless. They occur in a seemingly endless array of colors and sometimes change color as they mature. They grow on a wide variety of substrates, including soil, wood, conifer cones, fruits, straw, manure, and other mushrooms. Although some are known to be excellent edibles and some are known to be poisonous (including a few that are deadly), the edibility of the vast majority is unknown.

Agaricus campestris

Scientific name: *Agaricus campestris*

Common name: Meadow Mushroom, Pink Bottom

Key identifying features

1. Cap white to whitish, $1^1/_2$–5" wide, rounded and not distinctly flattened on the disc.

2. Gills pink, pinkish brown, or dark brown.
3. Gills of immature specimens covered by a white membranous partial veil that later forms a white ring on the stalk.
4. Stalk white, lacking a volva.
5. Stalk not staining yellow when bruised or scraped.
6. Flesh white, unchanging when exposed, lacking any distinctive odor.
7. Growing in grassy areas on lawns or pastures and not associated with trees.

Cap: 1–4" wide, convex to nearly flat in age; surface coated with tiny fibrils or nearly smooth, sometimes slightly scaly, dry, white to grayish or grayish brown; flesh white; odor and taste not distinctive.

Gills: free, crowded, pink when young, becoming dark brown in age.

Stalk: 1–2$^{3}/_{8}$" long, $^{3}/_{8}$–$^{5}/_{8}$" thick, nearly equal in size at all points, or enlarged or tapered at the base; smooth, white; partial veil membranous, white, leaving a sparse, persistent, or disappearing superior ring.

Spore print: dark brown.

Fruiting: scattered, in groups, or sometimes in clusters, arcs, or fairy rings on lawns, pastures, golf courses, and other grassy areas; June–September; common.

Edibility: edible and often rated choice.

Comments: The Horse Mushroom, *Agaricus arvensis*, edible, is similar but has a larger cap, up to 10" wide, a white stalk that soon stains yellow when bruised, and white flesh that has a distinctive anise- or almondlike odor (see p. 11). Also compare with the Eastern Flat-topped Agaricus, *Agaricus placomyces*, poisonous, which has white flesh with an unpleasant creosote or phenolic odor and a white stalk that stains yellow when bruised (see p. 66). The Destroying Angel, *Amanita virosa*, deadly poisonous, also has a white cap, but it has white gills that do not become brown in age, a universal veil that leaves behind a volva as the mushroom expands, a partial veil that tears and forms a ring on the stalk, and a white spore print (see p. 70).

Armillaria mellea

Scientific name: *Armillaria mellea*

Common name: Yellow Honey Mushroom, Honey Mushroom

Key identifying features

1. Cap yellow with a darker center.
2. Cap surface usually with tiny dark hairs.
3. Gills white to pale buff, covered when young by a thick partial veil.
4. Stalk with a conspicuous whitish ring.
5. Growing on the ground at the base of trees and stumps, or on decaying wood, usually in dense clusters.

Cap: $1^{1}/_{2}$–4" wide, convex to nearly flat, yellowish brown at first but soon becoming predominantly yellow with a darker center, sometimes dry but typically viscid, usually with tiny dark hairs, especially near the center of the cap, which may or may not be erect; flesh white, moderately thick at the center; odor and taste not distinctive.

Gills: attached to subdecurrent, typically with fine decurrent lines descending to the ring, white to pale buff; partial veil thick, membranous, whitish on the upper surface, yellowish on the lower surface, leaving a conspicuous whitish ring.

Stalk: 2–6" long, approximately $3/8$" thick, fibrous, often becoming scaly just below the ring, white at first, becoming yellowish to brown or olive in age, staining brownish where bruised; rhizomorphs flattened.

Spore print: pale cream.

Fruiting: in clusters on the ground, especially at the base of trees or stumps, sometimes directly on decaying wood; June-November; occasional to common.

Edibility: edible and good when thoroughly cooked.

Comments: The Yellow Honey Mushroom may be mistaken for the Deadly Galerina, *Galerina marginata,* deadly poisonous, which has a smaller, darker brown cap that lacks tiny hairs, a rusty brown spore print, rusty brown gills, and a small superior ring (see p. 76). Also compare with *Armillaria ostoyae* (see p. 30).

Descriptions: Edible Species

Armillaria ostoyae

Scientific name: *Armillaria ostoyae*

Common name: Brown Honey Mushroom, Honey Mushroom

Key identifying features

1. Cap dark reddish brown to yellowish brown or sometimes tan.
2. Cap surface usually with tiny dark hairs.
3. Gills white to pale buff, covered when young by a thick partial veil.
4. Stalk with a conspicuous whitish ring.
5. Growing on the ground at the base of trees and stumps or on decaying wood, usually in dense clusters.

Cap: 2–4" wide, convex, becoming broadly convex to nearly flat in age; dry; typically dark reddish brown, but sometimes tan to yellowish brown, densely covered with dark reddish brown to blackish scales; flesh firm, white, rather thick at the center; odor and taste not distinctive.

Gills: attached to subdecurrent, close, white to cream at first, becoming grayish orange to cinnamon; partial veil thick, membranous, leaving a whitish ring with a fluffy brown margin.

Stalk: 2–8" long, about $5/8$" thick at the apex, typically quite thickened downward at first, becoming cylindric in age, often distinctly tapered at the very bottom; fibrous, the fibers generally orangish to reddish brown; entire stalk staining mahogany to blackish when bruised; often with adhering bits of the partial veil; with yellow mycelial growth at the extreme base; rhizomorphs flattened.

Spore print: pale cream.

Fruiting: typically growing in large clusters, but sometimes solitary on the ground at the base of stumps or trees or on decaying wood; July-November; occasional to common.

Edibility: edible and good when thoroughly cooked.

Comments: The Brown Honey Mushroom may be mistaken for the Deadly Galerina, *Galerina marginata,* deadly poisonous, which has rusty brown gills, a rusty brown spore print, a small superior ring, and a smaller, smooth cap that lacks tiny hairs (see p. 76). Also compare with the Yellow Honey Mushroom, *Armillaria mellea,* edible (see p. 28).

Clitocybe nuda

Scientific name: *Clitocybe nuda*

Common name: Blewit

Key identifying features

1. Cap violet to lilac-gray or pinkish buff.
2. Flesh pale violet or lilac, often with an aniselike odor.
3. Stalk staining dark lavender when bruised.
4. Spore print pinkish buff.
5. Partial veil and ring absent.

Cap: $1^{5}/_{8}$–$5^{7}/_{8}$" wide, convex when young, becoming broadly convex to nearly flat in age; surface smooth, hygrophanous, slightly viscid and shiny when moist, dull when dry, sometimes finely cracked over the disc, with or without a low and broad umbo, violet to lilac-gray or pinkish buff, fading to pinkish tan or buff in age; margin inrolled when young, becoming expanded and occasionally uplifted in age, wavy, faintly striate when moist; flesh pale violet or lilac; odor fragrant, often resembling anise; taste not distinctive.

Gills: attached and notched, close to crowded, pale lavender to violet or lilac, becoming lilac-buff to brownish in age.

Stalk: $1^1/_8$–3" long, $^3/_8$–$1^1/_8$" thick, equal at all points, often bulbous or club shaped at the base, solid, dry, fibrillose to scurfy, whitish, pale violet or lavender, bruising dark lavender, becoming brownish in age.

Spore print: pinkish buff.

Fruiting: solitary or in groups or clusters on the ground under hardwoods and conifers, in meadows and lawns, on decaying vegetable matter, and near compost piles; August–November; fairly common.

Edibility: edible.

Comments: When collecting *Clitocybe nuda* for the table, avoid confusion with possibly poisonous similar *Cortinarius* species that have a rusty brown spore print and a spiderweblike partial veil.

Coprinus comatus

Scientific name: *Coprinus comatus*

Common name: Shaggy Mane, Lawyer's Wig

Key identifying features

1. Cap oval to cylindric at first, becoming broadly conic in age.
2. Cap white with a brownish disc, coated with coarse scales that are white to pale reddish brown.
3. Gills white at first, becoming pinkish, and finally black as the mushroom dissolves in age.
4. Stalk white, with a thin white inferior ring.
5. Scattered on soil, in grassy areas, or in wood chips.

Cap: $1^{1}/_{8}$–2" wide and oval to cylindric at first, becoming broadly conic to nearly plane and 2–$3^{1}/_{8}$" wide in age; fragile; surface dry, white with a brownish disc, coated with coarse scales that are white to pale reddish brown and usually darkest at the tips; flesh white at first, becoming black as the mushroom dissolves in age; odor and taste not distinctive.

Gills: attached at first, then free from the stalk; crowded; white, then pinkish, and finally black as the mushroom dissolves in age.

Stalk: 3–12" long, $^3/_8$–1" thick, enlarged downward to a bulbous base, sometimes rooting, hollow, glabrous to silky-fibrillose, white, fragile; partial veil white, submembranous, leaving a thin, inferior ring.

Spore print: black.

Fruiting: scattered, in groups, or sometimes in clusters in grassy areas, on soil, or in wood chips; May–November; common.

Edibility: edible.

Comments: The Alcohol Inky, *Coprinus atramentarius,* poisonous for some individuals, has a gray to gray-brown cap and often grows in clusters (see p. 74).

Lactarius volemus

Scientific name: *Lactarius volemus*

Common name: Voluminous-latex Milky

Key identifying features

1. Cap dry, smooth to finely wrinkled, dark orange-brown to cinnamon-brown at the center, paler orange-brown toward the margin.
2. Cap lacking concentric zones of alternating colors.
3. Flesh odor somewhat fishy.
4. Gills whitish to cream, bruising tawny-brown, immediately exuding a whitish latex when cut.
5. Latex does not become yellow after exposure to air.
6. Latex tastes mild, not peppery.
7. Stalk lacking a ring.

Cap: 2–4" wide, broadly convex, becoming nearly flat with a depressed center to broadly funnel-shaped in age; margin incurved at first, expanding and becoming uplifted at maturity; surface dry, pruinose to velvety when young, becoming smooth to finely wrinkled in age, dark orange-brown to cinnamon-brown at the center, paler orange-brown toward the margin, fading in age to pale orange-brown then honey-yellow; flesh thick, brittle, white, staining brownish when cut or bruised; odor not distinctive in very young specimens, soon becoming fishy as the mushrooms mature; latex copious, white, becoming creamy white then brownish or grayish and staining gills and flesh tawny-brown; flesh and latex taste mild.

Gills: attached to slightly decurrent, broad, close, often forked, whitish to cream, bruising tawny-brown.

Stalk: 2–4$\frac{1}{2}$" long, $\frac{1}{4}$–$\frac{3}{4}$" thick, nearly equal at all points or tapered at the base, solid, sometimes hollow in age, nearly smooth, pale orange-brown to dull orange.

Spore print: white.

Fruiting: solitary, scattered, or in groups on the ground in hardwoods or mixed woods; July-September; fairly common.

Edibility: edible.

Comments: The Corrugated-cap Milky, *Lactarius corrugis,* edible, is nearly identical but has a darker reddish brown, distinctly wrinkled cap (see p. 11).

Macrolepiota rachodes

Scientific name: *Macrolepiota rachodes*

Common name: Shaggy Parasol

Key identifying features

1. Open cap more than 3" wide, with white flesh showing between coarse grayish to brownish concentric scales.
2. Flesh white, staining orange then reddish brown when cut or bruised.
3. Gills white, staining brown when bruised.
4. Stalk enlarged downward, often with a bulbous base, white above the ring, brownish below.
5. Partial veil present covering the gills of young specimens, leaving a superior ring.
6. Stalk base lacking a volva.
7. Spore print white, not grayish green.

Cap: $2^3/_4$–8" wide, rounded to convex, becoming nearly flat in age; surface dry, initially smooth, forming coarse scales as the cap expands, cinnamon-brown, pinkish brown, or grayish with dingy white flesh between the scales, disc usually remaining uncracked and brown; margin often shaggy or ragged with veil remnants; flesh white, thick, staining orange then reddish brown when cut or bruised; odor and taste not distinctive.

Gills: free from the stalk, close, broad, white, staining brown when bruised or in age.

Stalk: $2-5^7/_8$" long, $^3/_8-^3/_4$" thick, enlarged downward, often bulbous, smooth, white on the upper portion, with various shades of brown on the lower portion; stalk flesh staining yellow-orange or saffron when cut or bruised; partial veil white, membranous, leaving a thick-edged, superior, movable ring.

Spore print: white.

Fruiting: solitary or in groups on the ground among leaves, conifer needles, and wood chips, as well as in gardens; September-November; fairly common.

Edibility: edible and good.

Comments: Also known as *Lepiota rachodes*. The Green-spored Lepiota, *Chlorophyllum molybdites,* poisonous, is quite similar, but its flesh does not stain when cut or bruised, its gills become greenish at maturity, and it has a grayish green spore print (see p. 72).

Pleurocybella porrigens

Scientific name: *Pleurocybella porrigens*

Common name: Angel's Wings

Key identifying features

1. Cap white, fan- to shell-shaped, with thin flesh.
2. Stalk absent or rudimentary.
3. Gills white, crowded, not serrate.
4. Growing on decaying conifer logs and stumps, especially on eastern hemlock.
5. Spore print white.

Cap: $1^{3}/_{8}$–4" wide, fan- to shell-shaped; smooth, white, often tinged yellowish in age; flesh very thin, white; odor and taste not distinctive.

Gills: white, narrow, crowded.

Stalk: absent or rudimentary.

Spore print: white.

Fruiting: single to in clusters on dead conifer wood, especially eastern hemlock; August-October; common.

Edibility: a good edible when fresh and abundant.

Comments: The Oyster Mushroom, *Pleurotus ostreatus* complex, edible, is similar but has a larger, whitish to pale brown or grayish cap and much thicker flesh (see p. 42). Several species of the genus *Crepidotus,* edibility unknown, are similar, but they have brown spore prints.

Pleurotus ostreatus complex

Scientific name: *Pleurotus ostreatus* complex

Common name: Oyster Mushroom

Key identifying features

1. Cap smooth, whitish to pale brown or grayish, fan- or oyster-shell-shaped.
2. Gills whitish, descending the stalk; gill edges not serrate.
3. Stalk short, lateral, whitish, often somewhat hairy.
4. Growing on decaying wood or along roots, usually in clusters.
5. Spore print white or pale grayish lilac.

Cap: $1^1/_2$–$7^1/_8$" wide, convex, fan- or oyster-shell-shaped, surface smooth, moist or dry but not viscid; color variable, dark brown, yellowish brown to grayish brown, pale gray, tan to yellowish buff, creamy white, or whitish; flesh white; odor sometimes aniselike, fragrant, fruity, or not distinctive; taste not distinctive.

Gills: decurrent, close to subdistant, white, grayish white or pale cream.

Stalk: eccentric, lateral, rudimentary, or absent; when present, up to $1^1/_2$" long and up to $1^3/_8$" thick; dry, solid, enlarged at either top or base or nearly equal at all points; often coated, at least near the base, with downy white hairs, white to dingy yellow.

Spore print: white, buff, cream, or pale grayish lilac (see Comments).

Fruiting: typically growing in overlapping clusters, sometimes scattered on logs, stumps, and standing trees, usually hardwoods; April-November; very common.

Edibility: edible and often rated as choice.

Comments: Species in this complex are highly variable, including variable spore prints, and often difficult to separate even with a microscope; however, all are edible. Angel's Wings, *Pleurocybella porrigens*, edible, is similar but smaller and whiter, and has much thinner flesh (see p. 40).

Giant Puffballs

Giant puffballs have a large rounded fruit body that measures 4–24" in diameter. They have a white to pale brown outer covering that feels like deerskin. Giant puffballs grow on the ground in woodlands or in grassy habitats.

Langermania gigantea

Alan Bessette with *Langermania gigantea*

Scientific name: *Langermania gigantea*

Common name: Giant Puffball

Key identifying features

1. Fruit body large (6–24" wide), more or less round.
2. Outer surface white to pale brown, smooth.
3. Interior solid, lacking any evidence of gills or a stalk.
4. Growing on the ground in woodlands or in grassy areas.

Fruit body: very large, usually 8–15" wide, but sometimes attaining a diameter of 20" or more; nearly round when young, often somewhat flattened and indented at maturity; attached to the ground by a thick, cordlike, basal rhizomorph.

Spore case: white to creamy white, smooth, soft, resembling deerskin; cracking irregularly in age.

Spore mass: white, soft, becoming yellowish to yellow-green and finally greenish brown as the spores mature.

Fruiting: solitary, scattered, in groups, or sometimes in fairy rings on the ground in woods, pastures, parks, golf courses, and brushy areas; July-October; fairly common.

Edibility: edible when the spore mass is white.

Comments: Also known as *Calvatia gigantea,* this puffball is commonly attacked at maturity by *Syzygites megalocarpus,* a gray mold. The Purple-spored Puffball, *Calvatia cyathiformis,* edible when the spore mass is white, forms a smaller rounded fruit body with a maximum diameter of 7". It has a pale brown spore case that becomes cracked on the upper portion, and it forms a white spore mass that becomes dull purple and powdery at maturity (see p. 12).

Hypomyces

Members of this group are fungi that parasitize and disfigure other fungi. They are also called *hyperparasites*. More than forty species are known to attack various gilled mushrooms, boletes, and polypores. *Hypomyces* produce very tiny flask-shaped to rounded sexual structures called *perithecia* in which sexual spores are produced. The perithecia are often partially embedded in the host tissue, and their protruding necks are responsible for the sandpaperlike texture that covers their hosts.

Hypomyces lactifluorum

Scientific name: *Hypomyces lactifluorum*

Common name: Lobster Fungus, Lobster Mushroom

Key identifying features

1. Fruit body orange to orange-red or yellowish orange.
2. Outer surface roughened with tiny sandpaperlike bumps.

3. Interior flesh white to whitish beneath the thin orange outer covering
4. Growing on the ground or among mosses.

Fruit body: orange to reddish orange, sometimes with whitish areas, roughened like sandpaper, growing over the surface of funnel-shaped to irregular caps, stalks, and deformed gills of host mushrooms; parasitized caps are typically dense, are often partially buried in conifer debris, measure $2-7^{7}/_{8}$" wide, and are white and firm within.

Fruiting: solitary, scattered, or in groups on the ground or among mosses, often partially buried, usually in conifer woods; July–October; infrequent to fairly common.

Edibility: edible, choice.

Comments: *Hypomyces lactifluorum* is a very popular edible mushroom, even though the identity of the host species is usually undetermined. The Russula Mold, *Hypomyces luteovirens,* edibility unknown, attacks *Russula* species and forms a yellowish green to dark green sandpaperlike coating that deforms the gills of its host (see p. 13).

Morels

Morels are hollow-stalked, single-chambered mushrooms with spongelike, conic to bell-shaped caps that have distinct pits and ridges. They are considered choice edibles.

Morchella esculenta

Scientific name: *Morchella esculenta*

Common name: Common Morel, Yellow Morel

Key identifying features

1. Cap spongelike or honeycombed with distinct ridges and pits.
2. Cap not brainlike to irregularly lobed.
3. Lengthwise section through the cap and stalk reveals a single continuous hollow chamber.
4. Lengthwise section through the cap and stalk does not reveal a multichambered interior.

5. Base of the cap is firmly attached to the stalk, not free and draped or flaring like a skirt.

Cap: $3/4$–$2 3/4$" wide, $3/4$–7" tall, oval to conic or somewhat cylindric, spongelike, hollow, divided into pits and ridges of variable color, continuous with the stalk below; pits round to elongated and irregular, gray to brown or yellowish; ridges anastomosing, whitish to grayish, yellow or yellow-brown.

Stalk: 1–$4 1/2$" long, $3/4$–$2 3/4$" thick, nearly equal at all points or enlarged (sometimes massively) toward the base; hollow; surface whitish, granular, often ribbed.

Fruiting: solitary, scattered, or in groups on soil in a variety of habitats: near dead elms, in old apple orchards, in burned areas, among mixed hardwoods, and sometimes under conifers; April-June; common.

Edibility: edible, choice; one of the most highly prized and sought-after mushrooms for the table.

Comments: *Morchella esculenta* has many additional common names, including Sponge Mushroom, Land Fish, Pine Cone Mushroom, and Honeycomb. The Half-free Morel, *Morchella semilibera,* edible and choice, is similar, but its cap is attached to the stalk about midway and flares below (see p. 14). The Brain Mushroom, *Gyromitra esculenta,* poisonous, is similar, but it has a multichambered cap with brainlike lobes and convolutions, and it lacks pits and ridges (see p. 64). The Saddle-shaped False Morel, *Gyromitra infula,* poisonous, has a saddle-shaped, smooth, reddish brown to brown cap and a hollow to chambered whitish to pinkish buff stalk (see p. 10).

Polypores

Members of this very large group of fungi form fruit bodies with small cylindric tubes on the underside of the cap. Spores are discharged through a tiny mouthlike opening at the end of each tube, called a *pore*. Each fruit body forms many tubes, each with a pore, which accounts for the name *polypore*. Most species grow on wood, but a few grow on the ground. Many polypores are hard and woody or corky to leathery, but some are fleshy to fibrous. The tube layer of a polypore usually does not separate cleanly and easily from the supporting cap tissue. Several species are excellent edibles if collected when they are young and tender. Although no polypores are known to have caused fatalities, most are inedible because of their woody texture. A similar group called boletes resembles polypores that grow on the ground and produce their spores in tubes. Most boletes grow on the ground, have a cap and stalk, and are soft and fleshy, and their tube layers are usually cleanly and easily separated from the supporting cap tissue.

Grifola frondosa

Scientific name: *Grifola frondosa*

Common name: Hen of the Woods

Key identifying features

1. Fruit body a large dense cluster of overlapping caps attached to a common stalk.
2. Caps gray to brownish gray, becoming dull dark brown in age.
3. Undersurface of caps not staining black when bruised.
4. Growing on the ground at the base of trees, usually oak, maple, or beech.

Fruit body: a large dense cluster of overlapping caps attached to branches arising from a short, thick, common stalk.

Cap: $3/4$–$3 1/8$" wide, fan- to petal-shaped, sometimes lobed, fleshy-fibrous, laterally attached to the stalk branch; surface smooth to finely matted and wooly, faintly to distinctly zoned, gray to brownish gray, becoming dull dark brown in age; margin thin, wavy.

Flesh: up to $1/4$" thick, fleshy-fibrous, white; odor nutty or not distinctive; taste not distinctive.

Pore surface: white to creamy white; pores angular.

Stalk: $3/4$–$1 3/4$" long, up to 4" or more thick, repeatedly branched, white.

Spore print: white.

Fruiting: solitary or in groups on the ground at the base of trees, especially oak and maple; August-November; fairly common.

Edibility: edible and choice.

Comments: Fruit bodies may attain a diameter of 24" or more. *Polyporus umbellatus,* edible and choice, forms a large overlapping cluster of circular, whitish to pale brown, depressed caps with centrally attached branches that grow on the ground near hardwoods. The Black-staining Polypore, *Meripilus sumstinei,* edible, is also similar and forms a large overlapping cluster of caps, but it has thicker shelflike caps and a white pore surface that stains black when bruised or in age (see p. 15).

Laetiporus sulphureus

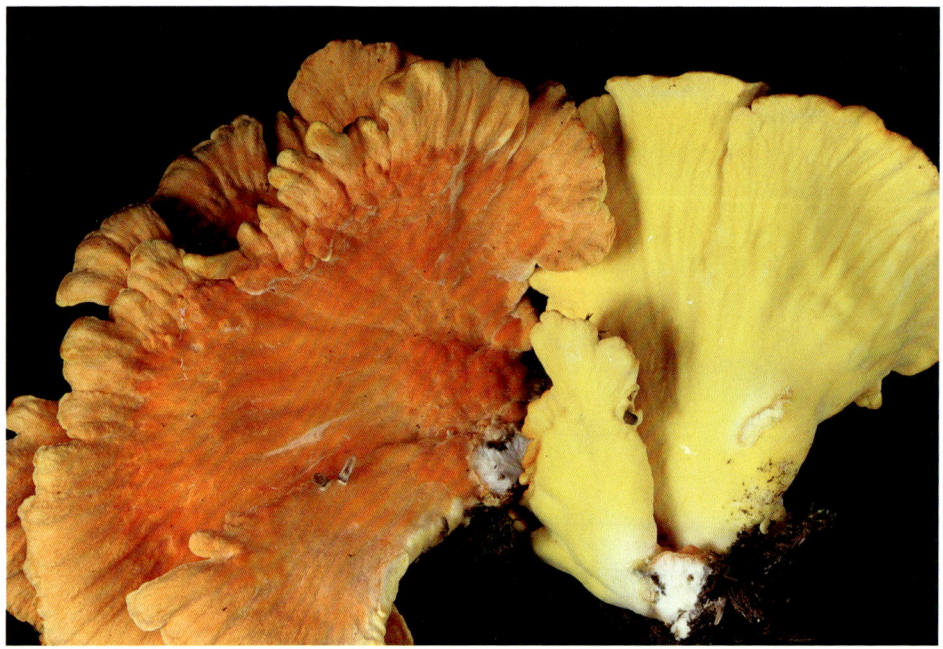

Scientific name: *Laetiporus sulphureus*

Common name: Chicken Mushroom, Sulphur Shelf

Key identifying features

1. Fruit body shelflike, stalkless, growing in overlapping clusters on trees, stumps, or logs.
2. Upper surface bright orange, smooth or wrinkled, velvety or densely matted.
3. Undersurface bright yellow with very tiny pores.

Fruit body: a large overlapping cluster of flattened, laterally fused, and lobed caps, sometimes forming rosettes or a solitary cap; stalkless or with a rudimentary stalk.

Cap: 2–12" wide, fan- to petal-shaped, soft, fleshy when young, fibrous tough in age; surface velvety to densely matted, dry, radially wrinkled, and roughened; bright to dull orange, fading to orange-yellow then whitish in age; margin pale orange, blunt, wavy, often lobed.

Flesh: up to ³/₄" thick, fleshy-fibrous, white; odor nutty or not distinctive; taste not distinctive.

Pore surface: bright sulfur-yellow; pores angular.

Spore print: white.

Fruiting: solitary, overlapping clusters, or rosettes on hardwoods, especially oak and cherry, occasionally on conifers, especially hemlock; May-November; fairly common.

Edibility: edible and choice when collected on hardwoods; may cause gastrointestinal upset when gathered from conifer wood, especially when consumed with alcohol.

Comments: The flesh of this mushroom has the consistency and flavor of white chicken meat.

Tooth Fungi

Members of the tooth fungi, also known as spine fungi, have downward-pointing, spinelike teeth on which they produce spores. Most tooth fungi grow on the ground and form teeth on the underside of their caps. Other members grow on wood and have teeth along branches or at the tips of branches. One species, usually found on standing trees, resembles a satyr's beard and has long spines hanging from a stalkless, unbranched, solid mass of tissue. The spinelike tips of similar coral fungi do not point downward. Several species are excellent edibles, but many others are much too tough to be eaten.

Hericium erinaceus

Photograph by Dail Dunaway

Scientific name: *Hericium erinaceus*

Common name: Bearded Tooth, Satyr's Beard

Key identifying features

1. Fruit body a whitish to yellowish, cushion-shaped, solid, branchless mass resembling a beard.

2. Long downward-oriented spines that taper to a point.
3. Growing on hardwoods.

Fruit body: $2^3/_4$–8" wide, $3^3/_4$–8" high, a whitish to yellowish, solid, cushion-shaped, branchless mass resembling a beard, giving rise to long spines; flesh thick, white, soft; odor and taste not distinctive when young, sour and unpleasant in age; spines $^3/_4$–$2^3/_4$" long, tapering to a point.

Fruiting: solitary on standing trunks or fallen logs of hardwoods; August-November; occasional to fairly common.

Edibility: edible.

Comments: The Comb Tooth, *Hericium coralloides,* edible, is a cluster of white, spreading branches with spines arranged in rows along the branches like teeth on a comb. The Bear's Head Tooth, *Hericium americanum,* edible, is a cluster of white, compact, forking branches with spines arranged primarily in bundles at the tips of the branches (see p. 16). Both species are similar to the Bearded Tooth, but differ by having much shorter spines that are borne on branches.

Hydnum repandum

Scientific name: *Hydnum repandum*

Common name: Sweet Tooth, Hedgehog

Key identifying features

1. Cap yellowish orange to pale brownish orange or reddish orange.
2. Undersurface of cap with downward-oriented whitish to orange-yellow spines.
3. Stalk white with orange tints or colored like the cap.
4. Growing on the ground under conifers or hardwoods.

Cap: $3/4$–6" wide, convex to nearly plane, sometimes slightly depressed, dry, felty, becoming somewhat wrinkled and pitted in age; yellow-orange, pale brownish orange to apricot-orange or reddish orange, staining dark orange when bruised; margin wavy, sometimes deeply indented or lobed; undersurface covered with spines, $1/8$–$3/8$" long, not decurrent or irregularly so; creamy white to orange-yellow, darkening when bruised.

Flesh: thick, firm, brittle; white, staining orange-yellow when cut and rubbed; odor pleasant, somewhat nutty to sweet or not distinctive; taste mild or sometimes peppery.

Stalk: 1–4" long, $^3/_8$–1$^3/_8$" thick, nearly equal at all points, solid, white with orange tints, or colored like the cap, bruising orange-yellow.

Fruiting: solitary, scattered, or in groups on the ground under conifers and hardwoods; July-November; common.

Edibility: edible.

Comments: A similar species, *Hydnum umbilicatum,* edible, is smaller and somewhat darker and typically has a distinctly depressed area at the center of its cap (see p. 16).

Descriptions and Illustrations of Inedible and Poisonous Species

Boletes

Boletes, also known as *fleshy pored fungi,* are among the most fascinating and highly prized mushrooms. Their beautiful colors, distinctive features, and relative abundance make them one of the most popular groups collected. Boletes are a relatively safe group to collect for the table and are immensely popular among mycophagists. Most boletes grow on the ground and are soft and fleshy. They have a cap, a stalk, and a spongelike layer of tubes on the undersurface of the cap. Each vertically arranged tube terminates in a pore. The tube layer is easily detached and typically separates cleanly from the cap flesh. Polypores also have tubes, but can easily be differentiated from boletes because most of the former grow on wood. The fruit bodies of polypores are typically tough and leathery to woody, and their tube layers usually do not separate cleanly from the cap flesh.

Boletes with an orange to red pore surface or with bitter-tasting flesh or with flesh that stains blue to grayish blue or greenish blue or blackish when cut or bruised must not be consumed.

Boletus subvelutipes

Scientific name: *Boletus subvelutipes*

Common name: Red-mouth Bolete

Key identifying features

1. Cap color variable, some shade of brown to reddish orange or orange-yellow.
2. Flesh yellow, quickly staining dark blue to blackish when cut or bruised.
3. Pore surface red or red-orange to orange, quickly staining dark blue to blackish when bruised.
4. Stalk base with short, stiff, dark red hairs.

Cap: $2^3/_8$–$5^1/_8$" wide, convex, becoming broadly convex to nearly flat; surface dry, finely velvety when young, occasionally finely cracked in age, color variable, cinnamon-brown to yellow-brown, reddish brown, or reddish orange to orange-yellow, quickly staining blue to blue-black when bruised; flesh yellow, quickly staining dark blue to blackish when cut or bruised; odor not distinctive, taste mild to slightly acidic.

Pore surface: red or red-orange to orange when fresh, duller in age, quickly staining dark blue to blackish when cut or bruised; pores circular.

Stalk: $1^1/_8$–4" long, $^3/_8$–$^3/_4$" thick, nearly equal at all points, solid, punctate with red dots or points, lacking a netlike pattern, quickly staining blue to blackish when bruised; with short, stiff, dark red hairs at the base on mature specimens (immature specimens often have yellow hairs that become dark red in age); partial veil and ring absent.

Spore print: dark olive-brown.

Fruiting: solitary to scattered on the ground under hardwoods, especially oak; June-September; fairly common.

Edibility: poisonous.

Comments: This mushroom causes mild to severe gastrointestinal upset when eaten.

Tylopilus felleus

Scientific name: *Tylopilus felleus*

Common name: Bitter Bolete

Key identifying features

1. Cap some shade of brown, buff, or tan.
2. Flesh white, not blueing when cut or bruised.
3. Flesh taste very bitter.
4. Pore surface white when young, becoming pinkish tan in age.
5. Stalk with a prominent dark brown netlike pattern.

Cap: 2–11 3/4" wide, rounded to convex, becoming broadly convex to flat; surface dry, smooth, sometimes sticky when moist, some shade of brown, buff, or tan; flesh white, not staining blue when cut or bruised; odor not distinctive; taste very bitter.

Pore surface: white when young, becoming pinkish or pinkish tan in age, not staining blue when cut or bruised, often staining brown; pores nearly circular.

Stalk: $1^1/_2$–$7^7/_8$" long, $^3/_8$–$1^1/_4$" thick, enlarging downward, bulbous, solid, entirely brown or white toward the apex and brown below, often developing olive or olive-brown stains when bruised, with a prominent dark brown netlike pattern at least over the upper one-third; partial veil and ring absent.

Spore print: pinkish brown, reddish brown, or rosy brown.

Fruiting: solitary or in groups on the ground or on decaying wood under conifers and mixed woods; June–October; common.

Edibility: inedible, bitter.

Comments: This mushroom is sometimes confused with the King Bolete, *Boletus edulis,* which has a whitish netlike pattern on its stalk and mild-tasting flesh (see p. 18). It is edible and choice for persons who lack the gene(s) for detecting bitter tastes.

False Morels

False morels have a brownish brainlike to irregularly lobed cap that is deeply wrinkled to convoluted. The interior of the cap is multi-chambered. These mushrooms have a dingy white to tan stalk that is often ribbed near the base.

Gyromitra esculenta

Scientific name: *Gyromitra esculenta*

Common name: Brain Mushroom

Key identifying features

1. Cap brainlike to irregularly lobed.
2. Cap lacking pits and ridges.
3. Lengthwise section through the cap reveals a multichambered interior.

Cap: $1^3/_8$–4" wide, $1^1/_2$–4" tall, brainlike to irregularly lobed, deeply wrinkled to convoluted, moist or dry; margin undulating to contorted, often curved toward the stalk; fertile surface pinkish tan to dark reddish brown or orange-brown, lubricous when fresh; sterile surface pale pinkish tan to yellowish tan.

Stalk: $3/4$–$2 3/4$" long, $3/4$–$1 1/8$" thick, enlarging downward or nearly equal, hollow or stuffed with cottony hyphae, sometimes chambered; surface smooth and waxy to slightly granular, dingy white to pinkish tan or tan, often ribbed near the base.

Fruiting: solitary, scattered, or in groups on the ground under conifers; April-June; common.

Edibility: poisonous; contains hydrazines, which can cause serious illness or death.

Comments: The interior of the cap is multichambered, and its flesh is very brittle. Many common names have been assigned to this mushroom, including Conifer False Morel, Beefsteak Morel, and Lorchel. Compare with the Common Morel, *Morchella esculenta*, edible, which has pits and ridges and lacks the brainlike lobes and convolutions (see p. 48).

Gilled Mushrooms

Gilled mushrooms belong to a very large group of fungi that have caps with knifebladelike gills on the undersurface. Many have a central stalk, whereas others are eccentrically to laterally stalked or stalkless. They occur in a seemingly endless array of colors and sometimes change color as they mature. They grow on a wide variety of substrates including soil, wood, conifer cones, fruits, straw, manure, and other mushrooms. Although many are known to be excellent edibles, and some are known to be poisonous (including a few that are deadly), the edibility of the vast majority is unknown.

Agaricus placomyces

Scientific name: *Agaricus placomyces*

Common name: Eastern Flat-topped Agaricus

Key identifying features

1. Cap surface covered with tiny grayish to grayish brown scales on a white background color.

2. Cap usually distinctly flattened on the disc.
3. Flesh white, odor unpleasant, like creosote or phenol.
4. Stalk white, staining yellow when bruised, often bulbous.
5. Gills pink to dark brown.
6. Growing on the ground in woodlands, in grassy areas with trees, or on sawdust piles.

Cap: $1-3^{1}/_{2}$" wide, convex, becoming broadly convex with a low and broad umbo, usually distinctly flattened on the disc; surface covered with tiny grayish to grayish brown scales on a white background color; disc grayish brown; flesh white; odor unpleasant, like creosote or phenol; taste unpleasant or not distinctive.

Gills: free, crowded, white at first, becoming pink and finally dark brown in age.

Stalk: $1^{3}/_{8}-4$" long, $^{1}/_{4}-^{1}/_{2}$" thick, nearly equal at all points down to a bulbous or sometimes abruptly bulbous base; smooth; flesh white, staining yellow in the base when cut and rubbed; partial veil membranous, white, with cottony patches, with or without brown droplets or brown stains on the unbroken undersurface, leaving a superior, single-layered ring with cottony patches on the undersurface.

Spore print: dark brown.

Fruiting: scattered or in groups on the ground in woods, especially among hardwoods, in grassy areas with trees, or on sawdust piles; June-September; fairly common.

Edibility: poisonous.

Comments: Compare with the Meadow Mushroom, *Agaricus campestris,* edible, which has a white stalk that does not stain yellow when bruised and white flesh that lacks a distinctive odor (see p. 26).

Amanita muscaria var. *formosa*

Scientific name: *Amanita muscaria* var. *formosa*

Common name: Yellow-orange Fly Agaric

Key identifying features

1. Cap yellow to orangish yellow, typically deeper orange on the disc, coated with whitish to pale tan warts.
2. Gills white to cream, covered by a partial veil when young.
3. Stalk enlarged downward with a pendant superior ring.
4. Growing on the ground under hardwoods or conifers.

Cap: $1^3/_4$–7" wide, convex to flat or slightly sunken at the center; pale yellow to orangish yellow, typically deeper orange on the disc and fading toward the margin; smooth, dry to sticky, margin distinctly striate; coated with numerous concentrically to irregularly arranged floccose whitish or pale tan warts; flesh thick, white.

Gills: free or very finely attached, crowded, rather broad, white to cream, sometimes slightly yellowish on the edges; partial veil white to yellowish, thin.

Stalk: $1^3/_4$–$6^1/_2$" long, $1/_4$–$1^1/_4$" thick, tapering slightly toward the top, white to pale yellowish, staining yellowish when handled, decorated with fine delicate fibers or small scales, sometimes rather roughened, stuffed; ring superior, pendant, white to pale yellow, membranous, thin but with a thickened edge, often disappearing; lower portion of stalk decorated with several whitish to pale yellowish ascending rings of universal veil tissue; bulb subglobose, sometimes with a very slight radicating point.

Spore print: white.

Fruiting: scattered to grouped, usually gregarious, on the ground in woods or under trees, usually near birch, poplar, or various conifers, especially white pine; July-October; very common.

Edibility: poisonous.

Comments: The Yellow-orange Fly Agaric is one of New York State's most common and conspicuous mushrooms, often fruiting in huge quantities.

Amanita virosa

Scientific name: *Amanita virosa*

Common name: Destroying Angel

Key identifying features

1. Cap white, lacking warts.
2. Gills white, covered by a white partial veil when young.
3. Stalk white, with a superior, pendant, white, membranous ring.
4. Stalk base enclosed in a white volva.
5. Growing on the ground in woodlands.

Cap: $1^{1}/_{8}$–$5^{1}/_{8}$" wide, convex to nearly flat, white, sometimes with a discolored center, smooth, dry to sticky, margin nonstriate; no warts present; staining yellow with potassium hydroxide (KOH); flesh white; odor and taste not distinctive.

Gills: free or very finely attached, crowded, white; partial veil white, thin, membranous.

Stalk: $2^3/_8$–8" long, $^1/_4$–$^3/_4$" thick, tapering slightly toward the top, white, smooth to roughened, solid; ring superior, pendant, readily adhering to stalk, white, membranous, thin and delicate, often torn; basal bulb small, usually fairly round; volva large, white, saccate, fairly thin, membranous, sometimes multilobed.

Spore print: white.

Fruiting: usually solitary, scattered, or in groups on the ground in mixed woods; June-November; common.

Edibility: deadly poisonous.

Comments: Several other similar species are also deadly poisonous and must be separated by microscopic examination.

Chlorophyllum molybdites

Scientific name: *Chlorophyllum molybdites*

Common name: Green-spored Lepiota, Green-spored Parasol

Key identifying features

1. Open cap more than 3" wide, white overall or with large brownish patches at maturity.
2. Cap and stalk flesh not staining when cut or bruised.
3. Gills white at first, becoming greenish to grayish green in age.
4. Partial veil present on the gills of young specimens, leaving a superior ring on the stalk.
5. Spore print green to grayish green.
6. Growing on the ground in lawns, meadows, or gardens.

Cap: $2^3/_4$–12" wide, round, becoming convex to nearly flat; surface dry, white, when young covered with large pinkish brown to cinnamon patches that become scalelike in age, usually clustered toward the disc; flesh white, thick, not staining when cut or bruised, or occasionally slowly staining reddish; odor and taste not distinctive.

Gills: free from the stalk, close, broad, white, becoming greenish to grayish green in age, staining yellow to brownish when cut or bruised.

Stalk: 4–10" long, $3/_8$–1" thick, nearly equal or enlarged downward, smooth, white, staining brownish when bruised; partial veil white, membranous, forming a superior ring with a fringed or double edge; ring becoming brownish on the underside in age, often moveable; flesh white, not staining when cut or bruised.

Spore print: green to grayish green.

Fruiting: solitary, scattered, or in groups or fairy rings in lawns, meadows, and gardens; August-October; infrequent.

Edibility: poisonous (see Comments).

Comments: This species is one of the most frequent causes of serious mushroom poisoning in eastern North America; its toxins can cause such severe vomiting that hospitalization is required to prevent acute, life-threatening dehydration. Although the Green-spored Parasol is very common in the southeastern United States, it is infrequently encountered in New York State. The Shaggy Parasol, *Macrolepiota rachodes,* edible, is similar, but it has white stalk flesh that stains yellow-orange or saffron when cut or bruised, white gills that do not become greenish at maturity, and a white spore print (see p. 38).

Coprinus atramentarius

Scientific name: *Coprinus atramentarius*

Common name: Alcohol Inky

Key identifying features

1. Cap gray to grayish brown, often with shallow grooves on the margin.
2. Gills very crowded, white at first, soon gray then black and dissolving into a black inky fluid in age.
3. Stalk white, with a white annular zone toward the base.
4. Growing in clusters in grassy areas, on wood chips, or at the base of trees.

Cap: $1^1/_2$–3" wide, oval to egg shaped when young, becoming convex in age; surface smooth to slightly scurfy, sometimes forming tiny scales on the disc, dry, gray to grayish brown, often with shallow grooves on the margin; flesh grayish white; odor and taste not distinctive.

Gills: free, very crowded, white when very young, soon gray, then black and dissolving into a black inky fluid in age.

Stalk: $1^1/_2$–6" long, $^3/_8$–$^3/_4$" thick, nearly equal or tapered downward, silky, hollow in age, white, with a white annular zone toward the base.

Spore print: black.

Fruiting: in clusters in grassy areas, on wood chips, or at the base of trees; May-November; very common.

Edibility: edible, with caution; see Comments.

Comments: Most people who consume this mushroom enjoy it without adverse reactions. However, some individuals experience coprine poisoning if they consume alcoholic beverages while, or up to forty-eight hours before or after, eating this mushroom. Signs and symptoms of coprine poisoning may include nausea, vomiting, marked flushing, rapid breathing, and severe headache. The Shaggy Mane, *Coprinus comatus,* edible, has a white cap with white to reddish brown scales and usually grows scattered or in groups (see p. 34).

Galerina marginata

Scientific name: *Galerina marginata*

Common name: Deadly Galerina

Key identifying features

1. Cap dark brown to dark amber, fading in age, smooth, lacking tiny hairs on the disc.
2. Gills brown, becoming rusty brown.
3. Stalk whitish to brownish with a small, membranous, superior ring.
4. Spore print rusty brown.
5. Growing on decaying wood.

Cap: $1-2^{1}/_{2}$" wide, convex when young, becoming nearly flat in age, with or without a low, broad umbo; surface viscid, moist, smooth, hygrophanous, dark brown to dark amber, fading to yellowish orange or buff, often remaining darker over the disc; margin translucent-striate when moist; flesh brownish to buff, thin; odor not distinctive to slightly farinaceous; taste not distinctive.

Gills: from attached to very slightly decurrent, close, broad, brown, becoming rusty brown.

Stalk: $1^1/_8$–$3^1/_2$" long, $^1/_8$–$^1/_2$" thick, equal at all points or slightly enlarged at the base, hollow, dry, smooth to slightly pruinose at the apex, covered with grayish white flattened fibrils over a brown to blackish brown ground color; base usually coated with white mycelium; partial veil white, membranous, leaving a small, persistent, membranous, superior ring.

Spore print: rusty brown.

Fruiting: scattered, in groups, or in clusters on decaying hardwood and conifer stumps and logs; May-October; fairly common.

Edibility: deadly poisonous.

Comments: Formerly known as *Galerina autumnalis,* this mushroom contains the same kinds of toxins that are found in deadly *Amanita* species and causes liver and kidney damage, coma, and death. Because it grows on wood, it is sometimes mistaken for the edible Honey Mushrooms, *Armillaria mellea* (see p. 28) and *Armillaria ostoyae* (see p. 30).

Omphalotus olearius

Scientific name: *Omphalotus olearius*

Common name: Jack O' Lantern

Key identifying features

1. Bright orange to yellow-orange smooth cap.
2. Cap edge uplifted and wavy in age.
3. Undersurface of cap with thin, decurrent, yellow-orange gills.
4. Typically fruiting in clusters on decaying wood or from buried wood.

Cap: $2^3/_4$–7" wide, convex when young, becoming nearly flat and shallowly depressed at the disc in age, often with a small umbo; surface dry, smooth, streaked with tiny fibrils, bright orange to yellow-orange, often stained reddish brown in age; cap edge uplifted and wavy in age; flesh white with an orange tint; odor not distinctive or somewhat unpleasant; taste not distinctive.

Gills: decurrent, close, narrow, thin, yellow-orange.

Stalk: 2–7" long, $1/4$–$7/8$" thick, nearly equal, tapered at the base, solid, dry, smooth, becoming scurfy in age, yellow-orange.

Spore print: whitish cream.

Fruiting: in clusters at the base of hardwood trees and stumps, especially oak, or on the ground attached to buried wood; July-November; fairly common.

Edibility: poisonous, causing gastrointestinal upset.

Comments: Fresh specimens often glow green in the dark. Compare with the Golden Chanterelle, *Cantharellus cibarius,* edible, which has forked, blunt, gill-like ridges on its undersurface and usually does not grow in large overlapping clusters (see p. 20).

Golden Chanterelles

The Culinary Mushroom

Guidelines for Eating Wild Mushrooms

Collecting and eating wild mushrooms can be a safe and enjoyable experience, but carelessness and taking chances can be fatal. Be aware that not all mushrooms are safe to eat and that many are poisonous. Follow these specific guidelines whenever you consume wild mushrooms:

1. Never eat a wild mushroom unless you are positive that it is an edible species.
2. Do not eat questionable or unknown mushrooms that animals may eat. Differences in their physiology may allow them to consume safely those mushrooms that are poisonous to humans.
3. Save one or two intact mushrooms in the refrigerator at least forty-eight hours after eating a species for the first time. These samples can be used as reference specimens in case adverse symptoms develop. Avoid consuming more than one species when trying any species for the first time.
4. When eating a new species of an edible mushroom for the first time, consume only a small portion and gradually increase the amount when you are certain that no adverse effects are produced.
5. Consume specimens only if they are fresh and free of larvae. Gastric upset may result from consuming spoiled or infested mushrooms, causing you to blame the mushrooms rather than the bacteria or larvae within them.
6. Avoid overeating. Some mushrooms are safe when consumed in moderate quantity, but may cause gastric distress when eaten in large amounts. Consuming edible mushrooms with large amounts of butter or excessive amounts of alcohol may produce unpleasant reactions.
7. Thoroughly cook all mushrooms. Some mushrooms contain gastrointestinal irritants that must be destroyed by cooking.

8. Do not pick mushrooms from contaminated habitats. Contaminants may accumulate in mushroom tissues. Areas to avoid when gathering mushrooms for the table include industrial areas, landfills, waste sites, crop fields, and chemically treated lawns or golf courses, as well as along highways and near railroad tracks.
9. Carefully examine each specimen in each collection to be sure that you have not accidently mixed poisonous or unknown species with edible ones.
10. Avoid the general rules of thumb or old wives' tales that abound regarding the edibility of wild mushrooms. Most rules of thumb are dangerous and may be deadly. Learn to identify a mushroom positively as an edible species before consuming it.

Preparing and Preserving Wild Mushrooms

While gathering mushrooms for the table, begin cleaning known edible species during the collecting process. Trim away debris with a knife and cut across the stalk base to check for larval tunnels. Discard any specimens that are infested with insect larvae. After returning home, use a soft brush to remove any remaining dirt. Washing mushrooms in water may cause them to become soggy and lose some of their flavor. A moist paper towel is normally all that is needed to remove persistent debris.

Mushrooms can be preserved using a number of techniques. Some of them include:

Refrigeration: Store mushrooms in waxed paper or in paper bags. Avoid plastic wrap and airtight containers that trap moisture and encourage spoilage. Refrigerated collections of fresh mushrooms will keep for about a week.

Drying: This technique is one of the oldest and easiest methods for preserving mushrooms, especially boletes. In fact, the flavor of many mushrooms is concentrated by drying. Cut mushrooms into approximately $1/2$" slices and place them in a commercial dehydrator over medium to low heat for twenty-four hours. An alternative method for drying is to string pieces of mushrooms on thread and hang them in a warm, dry, and well-ventilated area. Store dried collections in airtight containers. Place the containers in the freezer for two weeks to destroy any larvae that may have survived the drying process, then remove the containers and store at room temperature. When dried and stored properly, mushrooms will keep indefinitely. They can be ground into powder using a mortar and pestle and then added to soups, gravies, sauces, and many other foods. Dried specimens may be reconstituted by soaking them in warm water, broth, wine, or other liquids for about fifteen minutes.

Freezing: Some mushrooms are better preserved by freezing rather than by drying. Examples are the Hen of the Woods and the Chicken Mushroom. Boletes and gilled mushrooms also freeze well. There are several freezing techniques, but the easiest and most reliable is simply to sauté the cleaned and sliced mushrooms in butter or olive oil or in a mixture of butter and olive oil over medium to high heat for one to two minutes. Allow them to cool, then place both the mushrooms and any expressed liquid into freezer bags or containers. They will keep for up to one year. When cooking with frozen mushrooms, either thaw them and sauté until golden brown or simply add them unthawed directly to your sauces or soups, making certain to cook them thoroughly.

Cooking Wild Mushrooms

Several books have been written on cooking mushrooms. Some are listed in the "Recommended Reading" section. The many ways to cook mushrooms include sautéing, frying, baking, broiling, grilling, steaming, and blanching. Two simple techniques are:

Sautéing: One of the fastest and easiest ways to enjoy mushrooms is to sauté them in butter, margarine, or olive oil. Several methods can be used to sauté mushrooms. One is to sauté slices in butter over low to medium heat for approximately fifteen minutes or until all liquid has been evaporated. The mushrooms may be browned, but do not overcook them. Adding onion, garlic, or other seasonings can provide a delicious blend of flavors.

Grilling: Depending on their size, specimens may be grilled whole or sliced. Caps and stalks, or slices of each, may be basted with olive oil or mild to spicy sauces and grilled over an open fire. As an alternative, try marinating them before grilling. Mushrooms should be grilled until slightly brown and not placed too close to the heat source.

Wild Mushroom Recipes

We have included the following recipes as examples of some of the ways mushrooms may be used as important parts of appetizers or meals.

Baked Brie Pastries with Boletes

8 ounces Brie cheese, room temperature, cut into cubes with rind
$1/2$ teaspoon dried rosemary, crumbled
pinch cayenne pepper
1 egg, lightly beaten
1 cup coarsely chopped boletes
1 tablespoon olive oil
15 phyllo pastry sheets
1 cup (2 sticks) unsalted butter, melted

Sauté boletes in olive oil over moderately high heat until golden brown.

Using food processor, blend cheese until smooth.

Add rosemary, cayenne, egg, and sautéed boletes. Blend until smooth.

Butter large baking sheets. Place one phyllo sheet on work surface (keep remainder covered with slightly damp towel). Brush phyllo lightly with melted butter. Top with second phyllo sheet. Brush lightly with butter. Repeat with third phyllo sheet. Cut stacked, buttered phyllo lengthwise into $3^1/_2$" wide strips. Then cut crosswise into $3^1/_2$" wide squares. Place 1 teaspoon cheese filling in center of each square, gather corners together over center, and crimp firmly. Transfer to prepared sheets, spacing 1" apart. Brush tops lightly with butter.

Repeat process using phyllo sheets, butter, and filling.

Refrigerate at least one hour (can be prepared one day ahead).

Preheat oven to 350°F. Bake until crisp and golden brown, about twenty to twenty-five minutes. Cool five minutes. Serve warm.

Makes about sixty appetizers.

Chanterelles with Pasta and Greens

3 cloves garlic, minced
$1/4$ cup olive oil
3 tablespoons butter
1 pound chanterelles, cleaned and thickly sliced
$1/2$ teaspoon dried rosemary
$1/2$ pound sweet Italian sausage links, cut into 1" pieces
1 pound penne rigate or pasta of your choice
6 ounces fresh spinach (or greens of your choice), cleaned and coarsely chopped
$1/4$ cup freshly grated Pecorino Romano cheese, plus more to accompany the meal
freshly ground black pepper

In a deep skillet, melt butter with olive oil. Add garlic and sauté over medium to high heat until golden. Add chanterelles and continue cooking, stirring occasionally, until tender and most of the liquid has evaporated, about ten minutes. Add rosemary.

Remove from heat.

While cooking garlic and mushrooms, fry sausage pieces in a separate pan until well done. Remove from pan, drain, and add to mushroom/garlic mixture.

Bring a large pot of salted water to a boil, and cook the penne rigate until al dente. Drain well.

Add pasta and spinach to mushroom/sausage mixture. Add $1/4$ cup grated cheese and mix well. Add up to 1 tablespoon additional olive oil if needed. Add black pepper to taste.

Serve with additional black pepper and grated cheese. Goes nicely with fresh tomato-basil salad and a full-bodied red wine.

Serves four.

Wild Mushrooms and Asparagus Frittata

4 cups sliced wild mushrooms (morels, Honey Mushrooms, boletes)
2 tablespoons butter
1 small onion, finely chopped
2 large yellow bell peppers, cut into 1/4" strips
3 pounds fresh asparagus, trimmed and cut into 1/4" pieces
10 large eggs
1/2 cup heavy cream
1 tablespoon dried parsley
1 cup shredded Colby or Monterrey Jack cheese
1 1/2 teaspoons salt
1/4 teaspoon freshly ground black pepper

Butter a 13-by-9-by-2" baking dish. Preheat oven to 350°F.
Melt 1 tablespoon butter in a large skillet and cook bell peppers and chopped onion over medium to low heat until tender, about ten minutes.

In a separate skillet, melt remaining 1 tablespoon butter and sauté mushrooms over medium heat, stirring frequently, until tender and all liquid has evaporated.

Meanwhile, blanch asparagus pieces in boiling water for one minute. Drain in a colander, rinsing under cold water.

Beat eggs in a large bowl. Mix in cream, cheese, parsley, salt, and pepper. Add the asparagus, bell pepper mixture, and the mushrooms.

Pour into prepared baking pan. Bake for thirty to thirty-five minutes in the middle of the oven until golden and set. Cool.

Serves ten to twelve if accompanying a meal, or six to eight as a main course.

New Red Potatoes and Honey Mushrooms

1 $^1/_2$ pounds (about 12 medium-small) new red potatoes
4 strips bacon
1 large onion, diced
2–4 cups sliced Honey Mushrooms
salt
freshly ground black pepper

Wash potatoes and quarter or half the larger ones so they are all of a uniform size. Boil them in salted water until fork tender.
While potatoes are cooking, fry bacon in skillet until crisp, and then drain bacon strips on paper towels.
Sauté onion in bacon fat until lightly browned. Add mushrooms and sauté until all mushroom liquid is expressed and evaporated.

Drain potatoes in colander. Return to pot. Toss gently with onion-
    mushroom mixture. Crumble bacon and add to potatoes.
Season to taste with salt and pepper.
Serves four.

Curried Chicken of the Woods

3 tablespoons butter
3 tablespoons extra virgin olive oil
3–4 shallots, minced
3 cups very young Chicken Mushrooms, sliced into strips 2–3" long and $1/4$" wide
$1/4$ teaspoon curry powder
1 cup frozen baby green peas (optional)
$1/4$ cup dry white wine
1 cup (8 ounces) heavy cream
salt
roasted pistachios for garnish

In a large skillet, melt butter with olive oil over medium to high heat.
Add shallots and sauté until golden brown.
Add mushroom strips and continue cooking approximately five minutes, stirring frequently.

Add curry powder and mix well.
Add peas, if desired, and wine. When peas are heated through, or, if not using peas, when mixture is bubbling, add the cream. Simmer until thickened.
Salt to taste.
Serve over polenta, rice pilaf, or pasta of your choice, with pistachios sprinkled on top.
Serves four.

Gnocchi Carbonara with Wild Mushrooms and Ham

1 package Knorr Carbonara sauce mix
1 cup diced cooked ham
2 cups sliced mushrooms of your choice
2 tablespoons olive oil
1 pound gnocchi or pasta of your choice
4 scallions, green tops only, minced
garlic salt
freshly ground black pepper

Prepare carbonara sauce according to package directions.
Add ham; cover and keep warm over low heat.
Sauté mushrooms in olive oil over moderately high heat until all
    liquid has evaporated and mushrooms are golden brown.
    Season to taste with garlic salt.
While mushrooms are cooking, bring a large pot of water to a boil
    and cook gnocchi until al dente (follow timing on package).
    Drain well.

Serve gnocchi with carbonara and ham sauce, spooning mushrooms on top and garnish with minced scallions.
Add freshly ground black pepper to taste.
Serves four as a main course.

Shrimp and Shrooms with Creamy Pesto Sauce

1 package Knorr Creamy Pesto pasta sauce mix
2 medium to large King Boletes
2 tablespoons olive oil
About 20 jumbo shrimp shelled, deveined, and cooked
garlic salt
fresh snow pea pods for garnish

Prepare Creamy Pesto sauce according to package directions. Keep warm.

Clean and trim boletes. Slice lengthwise into $1/2$" slices. Heat olive oil in large skillet. Sauté mushrooms over medium to high heat until golden brown on both sides and all liquid has evaporated. Season to taste with garlic salt. Keep warm.

Blanch pea pods for one minute in boiling water. Arrange on four plates with shrimp and mushrooms. Top with Creamy Pesto sauce.

Serves four as an appetizer or side salad.

Glossary

Recommended Reading

Index to Common Names

Index to Scientific Names

Glossary

anastomosing: fusing to form a network
annular zone: a poorly defined ring
attached: joined to the stalk
basal: located at the base
base: the lowest portion of the stalk
buff: pale creamy gray to pale creamy yellow
bulbous: having a bulblike base
button: the young, developing stage of a mushroom
cap: the upper part of a mushroom, which supports gills, tubes, spines, or a smooth surface on its underside
central: attached to the middle of the cap
close: the spacing of gills halfway between crowded and subdistant
concentric: arranged in a circular pattern
conic: shaped more or less like an inverted cone
conifer: a cone-bearing tree; one that has needlelike leaves, such as spruce, fir, hemlock, or pine
conk: a hard and woody polypore
convex: curved or rounded like the exterior of a circle
coprine: an amino acid found in some mushrooms, which when consumed before, with, or after alcohol may cause nausea, vomiting, a flushed feeling, rapid breathing, and other signs and symptoms of poisoning
crossveined: having tiny veins that connect adjoining gills or veinlike ridges
crowded: having little or no space between the gills
cylindric: shaped like a cylinder
decurrent: descending or running down the stalk; a form of gill attachment
depressed: sunken
disc: the central area of the surface of a mushroom cap
distant: spaced widely apart
eccentric: away from the center
equal: having the same thickness over the entire length
farinaceous: having an odor of fresh meal or resembling cucumber
fertile surface: the spore-bearing surface
fiber: a hairlike structure present on the cap or stalk of some mushrooms

fibril: a tiny fiber
fibrillose: composed of fibrils
fibrous: composed of fibers
flesh: the inner tissue of a fruit body
free: not attached to the stalk
fruit body: the fleshy to hard reproductive structure of a fungus, commonly called a mushroom
gills: thin to thick knifebladelike structures on the cap undersurface of some mushrooms
glabrous: bald, lacking hairs or scales
gregarious: closely scattered over a small area
habitat: the substrate from which the mushroom grows, such as among sphagnum mosses, on wood, or on the ground
hydrazine: a colorless, corrosive liquid used in rocket fuel that is released from some mushrooms during cooking
hygrophanous: appearing water soaked when fresh, fading to a paler color as water is lost
hypha (pl. hyphae): threadlike filaments of fungal cells
incurved: bent inward toward the stalk
inferior ring: a ring located on the lower stalk surface
inrolled: bent inward toward the stalk and upward
KOH: potassium hydroxide, usually made up in a 3–5 percent concentration in water; used to test color reactions
lateral: attached to the margin of a cap
latex: a watery or milklike fluid that exudes from some mushrooms when they are cut or bruised
lorchel: a common name for *Gyromitra esculenta* and other false morels
lubricous: smooth and slippery
margin: the edge of a mushroom cap
mycelium: a mass of entangled microscopic, threadlike filaments, typically hidden in a substrate
mycophagist: a person who eats mushrooms
mycophile: a person who loves mushrooms and other fungi
mycorrhizal: having a mutually beneficial relationship with a tree or other plant
ochre: brownish orange-yellow
parasite: an organism that obtains its nutrients from a living host
partial veil: a layer of fungal tissue that covers the gills or pores of some immature mushrooms
patches: flattened pieces of universal veil remnants
pendant: hanging or draping

perithecium (pl. perithecia): a minute, flask-shaped structure containing spores
plane: flat
pores: the open ends of the tubes of a bolete or polypore
pore surface: the undersurface of the cap of a bolete or polypore, where the open ends of the tubes are visible
pruinose: appearing finely powdered
punctate: marked with tiny points, dots, scales, or spots
radicating: forming a rootlike extension in the ground
recurved: curved backward or downward
rhizomorph: a group of thick, ropelike strands of hyphae growing together as a single organized unit
ring: remnants of a partial veil that remains attached to the stalk after the veil ruptures
saccate: sheathlike or cup shaped
saprobe: an organism that lives off dead or decaying matter
scale: an erect, flattened, or recurved projection or torn portion of the cap or stalk surface
scurfy: roughened by tiny flakes or scales
serrate: jagged or toothed like a saw blade
spines: tapered, typically downward-pointing projections on a mushroom cap's undersurface
spore: a microscopic reproductive cell with the ability to germinate and form hyphae
spore case: a structure containing the spore mass in species of puffballs and their allies
spore mass: a dense layer of spores
spore print: a deposit of spores on a piece of paper or glass from a mushroom's gills, tubes, or other spore-producing structures
stalk: the structure that arises from the substrate and supports the cap or spore case of a mushroom
sterile surface: a portion that lacks reproductive structures
striate: having small, more or less parallel lines or furrows
stuffed: containing a soft tissue that usually disappears in age, leaving a hollow space
subdecurrent: extending slightly down the stalk
subdistant: gill spacing halfway between close and distant
subglobose: nearly round
submembranous: somewhat like a membrane
substrate: organic matter that serves as a food source for a fungal mycelium

superior ring: a ring located on the upper stalk surface

tawny: dull yellowish brown

teeth: spines that point downward

tiers: nearly parallel rows

tubes: narrow, parallel, spore-producing cylinders on the undersurface of a bolete's or polypore's cap

umbo: a pointed or rounded elevation at the center of a mushroom cap

universal veil: a layer of fungal tissue that completely encloses immature stages of some mushrooms

veil: a layer of fungal tissue that covers all or part of some immature mushrooms (see *universal veil* and *partial veil*)

viscid: sticky or tacky

volva: a typically cuplike sac that remains around the base of a mushroom stalk when the universal veil ruptures

warts: small patches of tissue that remain on the top of a mushroom cap when the universal veil ruptures

Recommended Reading

Bessette, A. E. 1988. *Mushrooms of the Adirondacks: A Field Guide.* Utica, N.Y.: North Country Books.

Bessette, A. E., A. R. Bessette, and D. W. Fischer. 1997. *Mushrooms of Northeastern North America.* Syracuse, N.Y.: Syracuse Univ. Press.

Bessette, A. E., O. K. Miller, A. R. Bessette, and H. H. Miller. 1995. *Mushrooms of North America in Color: A Field Guide Companion to Seldom-Illustrated Fungi.* Syracuse, N.Y.: Syracuse Univ. Press.

Bessette, A. E., W. C. Roody, and A. R. Bessette. 1999. *North American Boletes: A Guide to the Fleshy Pored Mushrooms.* Syracuse, N.Y.: Syracuse Univ. Press.

Bessette, A. E., and W. J. Sundberg. 1987. *Mushrooms: A Quick Reference Guide to Mushrooms of North America.* New York: Macmillan.

Bessette, A. R., and A. E. Bessette. 1993. *Taming the Wild Mushroom: A Culinary Guide to Market Foraging.* Austin: Univ. of Texas Press.

———. 2001. *The Rainbow Beneath My Feet: A Mushroom Dyer's Field Guide.* Syracuse, N.Y.: Syracuse Univ. Press.

Bessette, A. R., A. E. Bessette, and W. J. Neill. 2001. *Mushrooms of Cape Cod and the National Seashore.* Syracuse, N.Y.: Syracuse Univ. Press.

Czarnecki, J. 1986. *Joe's Book of Mushroom Cookery.* New York: Atheneum.

Fischer, D. W., and A. E. Bessette. 1992. *Edible Wild Mushrooms of North America: A Field to-Kitchen Guide.* Austin: Univ. of Texas Press.

Index to Common Names

Page number in *italic* denotes illustration.

Alcohol Inky, 35, *74*
Angel's Wings, *40*, 43

Beafsteak Morel, 65
Bearded Tooth, *54*, 55
Bear's Head Tooth, 55
Bitter Bolete, 19, *62*
Black-staining Polypore, 51
Black Trumpet, *22*
Blewit, *32*
Brain Mushroom, 49, *64*
Brown Honey Mushroom, *30*, 31

Cep, *18*
Chicken Mushroom, *52*, 92
Cinnabar-red Chanterelle, 21
Comb Tooth, 55
Common Morel, *48*, 65
Connifer False Morel, 65
Corrugated-cap Milky, 37
Crown-tipped Coral, *24*

Deadly Galerina, 29, 31, *76*
Destroying Angel, 27, *70*

Eastern Flat-topped Agaricus, 27, *66*

Giant Puffball, *44*
Golden Chanterelle, *20*, 79
Green-spored Lepiota, 39, *72*
Green-spored Parasol, *72*

Half-free Morel, 49
Hedgehog, 56
Hen of the Woods, *50*, 51
Honeycomb, 49
Honey Mushroom, *28*, *30*, 77, 90
Horse Mushroom, 27

Jack O'Lantern, 21, *78*

King Bolete, ii, *18*, 63

Land Fish, 49
Lawyer's Wig, *34*
Lobster Fungus, *46*
Lobster Mushroom, *46*
Lorchel, 65

Meadow Mushroom, *26*, 67

Oyster Mushroom, 41, *42*

Pine Cone Mushroom, 49
Pink Bottom, *26*
Porcini, *18*
Purple-spored Puffball, 45

Red-mouth Bolete, 19, *60*
Russula Mold, 47

Saddle-shaped False Morel, 49
Satyr's Beard, *54*
Shaggy Mane, *34*, 75
Shaggy Parasol, ii, *38*, 73
Smooth Chanterelle, 21
Sponge Mushroom, 49
Sulphur Shelf, *52*
Sweet Tooth, 56

Voluminous-latex Milky, *36*

Yellow Honey Mushroom, *28*, 29, 31
Yellow Morel, *48*
Yellow-orange Fly Agaric, *68*, 69

Index To Scientific Names

Genus and species names are in *italic*.
Page number in *italic* denotes illustration.

Agaricus
    arvensis, 11, *27*
    campestris, *26*, 67
    placomyces, 27, *66*
Amanita
    muscaria, var. *formosa*, *68*
    virosa, 27, *70*
Armillaria
    mellea, 28, 31, *77*
    ostoyae, 29, *30*, *77*

Boletus
    edulis, 7, 18, *63*
    subvelutipes, 19, *60*

Calvatia
    cyathiformis, 12, *45*
    gigantea, 45
Cantharellus
    cibarius, 20, *79*
    cinnabarinus, 8, *21*
    lateritius, 8, *21*
Chlorophyllum molybdites, 39, *72*
Clavicorona pyxidata, 9, *24*
Clitocybe nuda, *32*, 33
Coprinus
    atramentarius, 35, *74*
    comatus, 34, *75*
Craterellus fallax, *22*

Galerina
    autumnalis, 77
    marginata, 29, 31, *76*
Grifola frondosa, 50
Gyromitra
    esculenta, 10, 49, *64*
    infula, 10, *49*

Hericium
    americanum, 16, *55*
    coralloides, 55
    erinaceus, *54*
Hydnum
    repandum, 56
    umbilicatum, 16, *57*
Hypomyces
    lactifluorum, 13, *46*, 47
    luteovirens, 13, *47*

Laetiporus sulphureus, 15, *52*
Lactarius
    corrugis, 11, *37*
    volemus, *36*
Langermania gigantea, 12, *44*
Lepiota rachodes, 39

Macrolepiota rachodes, 38, *73*
Meripilus sumstinei, 15, *51*
Morchella
    esculenta, 14, 48, *49*, *65*
    semilibera, 14, *49*

Omphalotus oleareus, 21, *78*

Pleurocybella porrigens, 40, *43*
Pleurotus ostreatus, 41, *42*
Polyporus umbellatus, 51

Ramaria concolor, 9, *25*

Syzygites megalocarpus, 45

Tylopilus felleus, 7, 19, *62*

Alan E. Bessette is a mycologist and professor of biology at Utica College of Syracuse University. He has published numerous professional papers in the field of mycology and has authored or coauthored fourteen books, including *Edible and Poisonous Mushrooms of New York; Mushrooms of the Adirondacks; Mushrooms: A Quick Reference Guide to Mushrooms of North America; Edible Wild Mushrooms of North America; Mushrooms of Northeastern North America;* and *North American Boletes: A Guide to the Fleshy Pored Mushrooms.* He has presented numerous mycological programs, is the scientific advisor to the Mid-York Mycological Society, and serves as a consultant for the New York State Poison Control Center. He has been the principal mycologist at national and regional forays and was the recipient of the 1987 Northeast Mycological Foray Service Award and the 1992 North American Mycological Association Award for Contributions to Amateur Mycology.

Arleen R. Bessette is a mycologist and botanical photographer who has been collecting and studying wild mushrooms for more than thirty years. She has authored or coauthored seven books, including: *Taming the Wild Mushroom: A Culinary Guide to Market Foraging; Mushrooms of North America in Color; Mushrooms of Northeastern North America,* and *Mushrooms of Cape Cod and the National Seashore.* Her most recent book is *The Rainbow Beneath My Feet: A Mushroom Dyer's Field Guide.* She has won several national awards for her photography and teaches introductory courses in mycology and mushroom cooking, as well as mushroom-dyeing workshops for the North American Mycological Association and other organizations.